Top 10 Worst

Murderous

Mythical Creatures

you wouldn't want to meet!

iFerocious

Yuck!

Author:
Fiona Macdonald studied history at Cambridge
University, England, and at the University of East
Anglia. She has taught in schools, adult education
and universities, and is the author of numerous
books for children.

Artist:
David Antram was born in Brighton, England, in
1958. He studied at Eastbourne College of Art and
then worked in advertising for fifteen years before
becoming a full-time artist. He has illustrated many
children's non-fiction books.

Series creator:
David Salariya was born in Dundee, Scotland.
He has illustrated a wide range of books and has
created and designed many new series for
publishers in the UK and overseas. In 1989 he
established The Salariya Book Company. He lives
in Brighton with his wife, illustrator Shirley Willis,
and their son Jonathan.

Editor: Jamie Pitman

Editorial assistants: Rob Walker, Mark Williams

Additional artwork:
Mark Bergin, Giovanni
Caselli, Pam Hewetson

Published in Great Britain in MMX by
Book House, an imprint of
The Salariya Book Company Ltd
25 Marlborough Place, Brighton BN1 1UB
www.salariya.com
www.book-house.co.uk

HB ISBN-13: 978-1-907184-40-6
PB ISBN-13: 978-1-907184-41-3

SALARIYA

1 3 5 7 9 8 6 4 2
A CIP catalogue record for this book is available
from the British Library.

Printed and bound in China.

PAPER FROM
SUSTAINABLE
FORESTS

Splash!

Top 10 Worst

Murderous

Mythical Creatures

you

wouldn't

want to

meet!

Grrrrr!

Yuck!

Illustrated by
David Antram

BOOK
HOUSE

Written by
fiona Macdonald

Created & designed by
David Salariya

Contents

Mythical mysteries

Myths are stories with meanings. They can be true and false, funny and serious, and frightening and comforting all at the same time. In myths you will meet gods and heroes, villains and victims, the brave and the beautiful – together with the strange, the silly, and the very, very scary.

I always wanted to be famous!

fantastic and fabulous

Myths feature many fantastic and fabulous animals. These mythical creatures are magical, mysterious, marvellous – but beware! They are not always friendly… Ammut? She'll gobble you up! Grendel? He'll tear you limb from limb! The Troll? He'll crunch your bones! The shining Winged Serpent brings death; horrid Baba-Yaga chases children. Even the Ancient Greek centaurs (part human, part horse) have a nasty side to them!

Voices from the past

Most myths are thousands of years old. They record ancient history and preserve old customs and beliefs. Until around 1800, many myths were never written down. Instead, they were memorised by generations of story-tellers and passed on by word of mouth.

Shudder!

Tremble!

Oooooh!

Eeek!

Shiver!

6

A world of wonders

Weird and wonderful creatures are found in myths from all round the world.

Thunderbird
(North America)

Kraken
(North Atlantic
and Arctic Oceans)

Werewolf
(North America
& Europe)

Mermaid
(Worldwide)

Most mythical creatures are the stuff of nightmares. So why do we like them? Because they are exciting and have amazing adventures? Because they inspire us to create our own games and fantasies? Or because their stories help us to cope with real-life scary feelings?

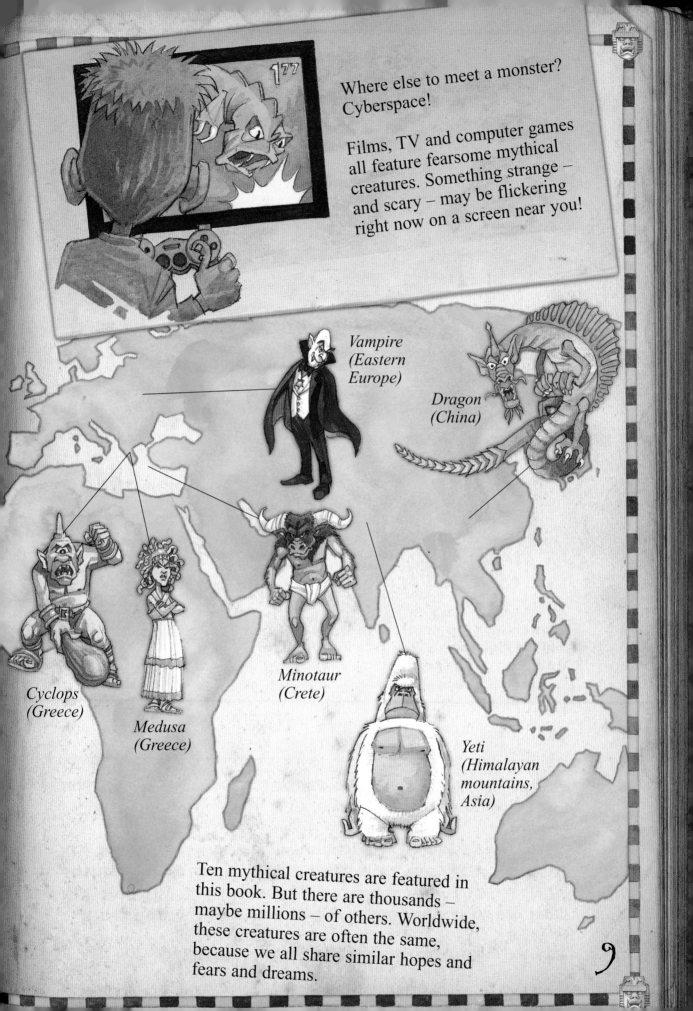

Where else to meet a monster? Cyberspace!

Films, TV and computer games all feature fearsome mythical creatures. Something strange – and scary – may be flickering right now on a screen near you!

Vampire
(Eastern Europe)

Dragon
(China)

Cyclops
(Greece)

Medusa
(Greece)

Minotaur
(Crete)

Yeti
(Himalayan mountains, Asia)

Ten mythical creatures are featured in this book. But there are thousands – maybe millions – of others. Worldwide, these creatures are often the same, because we all share similar hopes and fears and dreams.

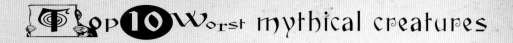

№o 10

Thunderbird

Listen! Can you hear him? Thunderbird is coming! Swooping down from his home in the sky, he brings wild winds in his wings. Thunderclaps shake the world whenever he flaps his feathers. When he blinks, lightning flashes from his eyes. Don't anger him or he'll send floods and storms to destroy you!

Whoosh!

Whoosh

Vital statistics

Name:	Thunderbird
Appearance:	Multicoloured eagle
Size:	Wingspan wide as two canoes
Armed with:	Beak, horns, talons
Home:	North America
Powers:	Brings violent storms

You wouldn't want to know this:

Thunderbird carries deadly snakes – like forked lightning – under his wings.

Today's weather forecast is mild, with showers of DEATH and DESTRUCTION!

Crackle!

Be prepared!
Always expect the very worst

Thunderbird vs. whale

Once, a monster whale devoured all the fish in the sea. Everyone was starving! Thunderbird attacked the whale, and they fought a terrible battle. Thunderbird won, and hurled the whale deep down into the ocean (where it still lives). Or else, some say, he carried it up to his lair and ate it!

Sign of strength

With its mighty wings spread wide, a carved Thunderbird keeps watch at the top of a tall totem pole in Canada. He's a sign of strength, an honoured ancestor, and a guardian.

Thunderbird lives among the clouds, at the top of a holy mountain.

Revenge of the Roc

Look out! Here it comes: the Roc, another giant bird, from Asia. It carries its lunch – an elephant! – and is ready to sink ships by dropping huge boulders onto them!

Help! Put me down!

№ 9

Mermaid

Pretty but deadly, mermaids kill by mistake. They sit smiling sweetly on jagged rocks, beckoning sailors to jump from passing ships to join them. Or they clasp sailors in their loving arms and take them to mermaid palaces underwater. Either way, the sailors drown, of course…

Vital statistics

Name: Mermaid
Appearance: Half woman, half fish
Size: Up to 61 metres (200 feet) long
Armed with: Sweet voice, long hair (sometimes green!), pretty face
Home: Rocky shores
Powers: Fatal charm

You wouldn't want to know this:

Seeing a mermaid brings dreadful disaster.

There are mermen, too, but they don't wreck ships or kill sailors.

I hope they stick around a bit longer this time!

Be prepared!
Always expect the very worst

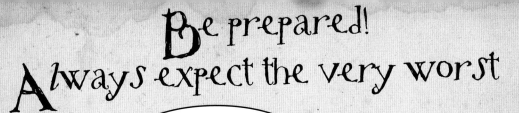

"You seem to have made a mer~stake!"

Mistaken identity

This gentle sea-creature has an appealing face and a friendly, inquisitive nature. But no, it's not a mermaid, as past sailors supposed. It's a real-life sea-cow, or manatee!

Spirit of the waters

You may see Mami Wata gliding through West African waves, or admiring her face in a mirror. But whenever you meet her, beware! Her brilliant jewellery can blind you!

Sinister singers

Sirens were monstrous sisters (half bird, half girl) who made the best music in the world. But hearing their songs lured sailors onto dangerous rocks – and then the Sirens devoured them!

Sparkle!

Tra~la~la!

The Sirens sang in Ancient Greece, over two thousand years ago.

13

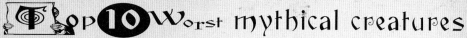

No 8

Cyclops

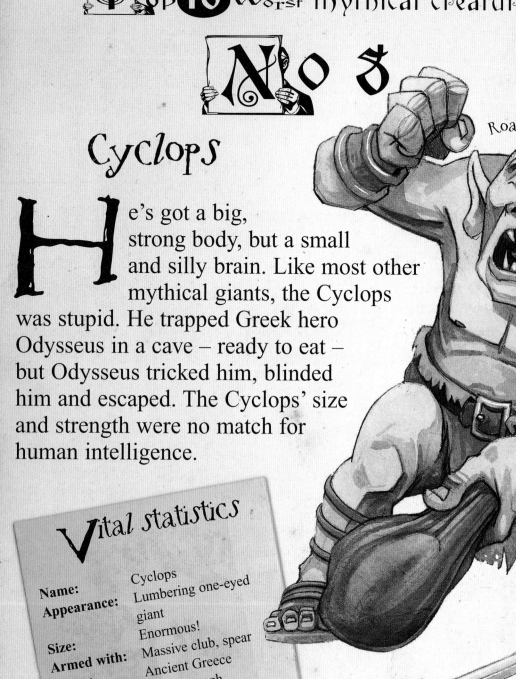

Roar!

He's got a big, strong body, but a small and silly brain. Like most other mythical giants, the Cyclops was stupid. He trapped Greek hero Odysseus in a cave – ready to eat – but Odysseus tricked him, blinded him and escaped. The Cyclops' size and strength were no match for human intelligence.

Vital statistics

Name: Cyclops
Appearance: Lumbering one-eyed giant
Size: Enormous!
Armed with: Massive club, spear
Home: Ancient Greece
Powers: Brute strengh

You wouldn't want to know this:

The Cyclops was a cannibal. He scooped up men and ate them, alive!

Har har!

The giant Goliath was three metres tall. The story of David and Goliath appears in the Bible.

Be prepared!
Always expect the very worst

I think I'll buy myself a big, sharp axe . . .

Gleam!

Sniff, sniff, sniff!

In the fairytale, Young Jack climbed a tall beanstalk to reach a giant's castle. But the giant was greedy, ravenously hungry, and had a very keen sense of smell! How did Jack escape? The giant's wife took pity on him, and helped him.

Record breaker

There are giants in the real world, as well as in myths and fairytales. Sultan Kosen (born 1982), a farmer from Turkey, holds the world record as today's tallest man.

Sultan Kosen (on the right) is 2.47 m (8 ft 1 in) tall.

Giant-killer

For forty days, the giant warrior Goliath challenged the Israelites. But no-one dared fight him – except for young David. He killed Goliath with just one pebble, hurled from a sling.

Take this!

No 9

Kraken

Deep in the ocean lurks a mighty monster: Kraken. Big as an island! Looks like a giant squid! Its huge bulging body makes fearsome whirlpools as it swims along, and its waving tentacles can pull the largest ships to the bottom of the sea.

Vital statistics

Name: Kraken
Appearance: Like a giant squid
Size: 20 metres or more
Armed with: Tentacles, sharp beak
Home: Atlantic and Arctic Oceans
Powers: Wrecks ships, drowns sailors

You wouldn't want to know this:

Kraken swallows small fish and belches them up, before eating the bigger fish that come to feast on the vomit. Yuk!

Help! The Kraken's crackin' the ship!

Splash!

Be prepared!
Always expect the very worst

Colossal squid

Real-life monster the colossal squid is 14 m (46 ft) long. It has tentacles covered with sharp hooks and the largest eyes of any living creature.

Colossal squid

Gargle!

Sperm whale

Giant eye

Tentacles

Predator X

Chomp!

What is the deadliest creature ever to have swum in the sea? It's 'Predator X', a fossil pliosaur (prehistoric reptile) discovered in 2008. It is 147 million years old. It was an immense 15 m (49 ft) long and had incredibly strong jaws and horribly sharp teeth.

Mega-monster

He makes the sea boil! He leaps up to eat the Sun! And, according to Bible stories, the proud and fearless Leviathan is the biggest creature on Earth.

> Sure I'm big but that doesn't make me bad!

17

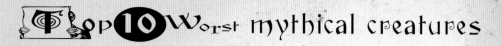

The Minotaur

The Minotaur had the mind of a man trapped inside the lumbering body of a bull. He was tragic and terrible, fierce and furious, neither man nor beast, but a mixture of both. His mother's husband, King Minos of Crete, had a special maze built to hide him, called the Labyrinth.

Snort!

Bull's head and horns

Vital statistics

Name: Minotaur
Appearance: Part human, part bull
Size: Like a mighty man
Armed with: Superhuman strength
Home: Crete, a Greek island
Powers: Preyed on human flesh

You wouldn't want to know this:

Seven girls and seven boys were fed to the minotaur every year.

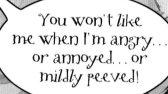

You won't like me when I'm angry... or annoyed... or mildly peeved!

Man's body

Be prepared!
Always expect the very worst

Wrestle!

Fair face, foul heart

Like the Minotaur, the Manticore was a hybrid (a mixture of more than one animal). It had a human head, a lion's body and a poisonous scorpion's tail. It looked good, but was deadly.

Grrr!

The Manticore was a symbol of the bad side of human nature.

Killer hero

Not only the son of a Greek god but a prince, athlete and dancer to boot, Theseus entered the Labyrinth, trailing thread behind him. He killed the Minotaur, then followed the thread out again. He was the only man ever to leave the Labyrinth alive.

Painting of bull-dancers from King Minos' palace, made around 2000 BC.

The dance of death

Seize a fierce bull by the horns, then somersault over its back. Landed safely? You're lucky! Gored to death? You're a human sacrifice to the Greek gods!

19

№ 5

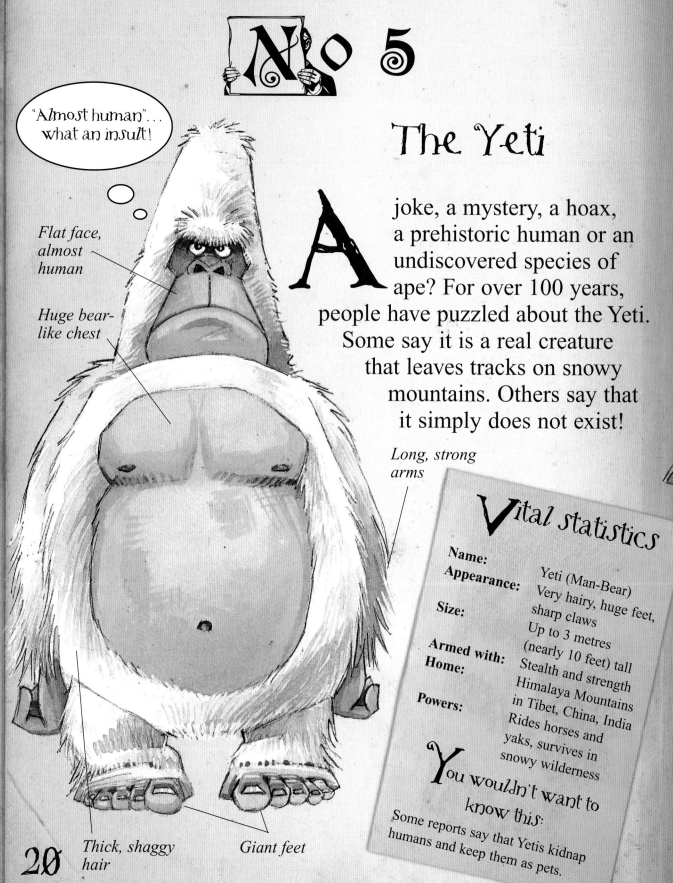

**"Almost human"...
what an insult!**

Flat face, almost human

Huge bear-like chest

Long, strong arms

Thick, shaggy hair

Giant feet

The Yeti

A joke, a mystery, a hoax, a prehistoric human or an undiscovered species of ape? For over 100 years, people have puzzled about the Yeti. Some say it is a real creature that leaves tracks on snowy mountains. Others say that it simply does not exist!

Vital statistics

Name: Yeti (Man-Bear)

Appearance: Very hairy, huge feet, sharp claws

Size: Up to 3 metres (nearly 10 feet) tall

Armed with: Stealth and strength

Home: Himalaya Mountains in Tibet, China, India

Powers: Rides horses and yaks, survives in snowy wilderness

You wouldn't want to know this:

Some reports say that Yetis kidnap humans and keep them as pets.

Be prepared!
Always expect the very worst

Early explorers

Since 1832, European explorers in the Himalayan mountain range of Asia have reported sightings of a strange wild creature that left mysterious tracks in the snow.

Bigfoot

What leaves footprints over 60 cm (2 ft) long and 20 cm (8 inches) wide? 'Bigfoot': a monster like the Yeti that is said to live in the North-West of North America.

Several people claim to have seen Bigfoot. Film footage showing a huge, hairy creature, almost 3 m (10 ft) tall, was recorded in California in 1967. But who knows whether the pictures were fake or real?

lurk!

No way am I going back up there!

Under the microscope

Imagine the excitement when explorers found clumps of 'Yeti' hair in a Tibetan monastery! But in 2008, scientists proved that the hair came from a goral. A goral is a Himalayan animal rather like a goat. What a disappointment!

At last I can *sleep safe* at night!

21

№ 4

Werewolf

What would it be like to change shape, to be transformed into an animal? That's what happens to werewolves, mostly at full moon. One minute, they're a normal person, the next, they have hairy skin, huge fangs, slavering jaws – and a hunger for dead bodies!

Vital statistics

Name: Werewolf
Appearance: Wolf standing upright like a human
Size: Large, lean, hungry wolf
Armed with: Sharp fangs and strong jaws
Home: Europe and North America
Powers: Kills; eats corpses; steals children

You wouldn't want to know this:

Women werewolves have poisonous claws – and can kill children just by looking at them!

Howwwl! Grrrrr! Snarrrl!

It is said that a werewolf can only be killed by a silver bullet.

Be prepared!
Always expect the very worst

Spot a werewolf: handy checklist

- Curved fingernails

- Ears low on head

- Eyebrows meet over the nose

- Bristles under the tongue

Hmm, should I see a doctor or eat one?

How to become a werewolf

- Be bitten by a werewolf
- Rub body with magic ointment
- Drink special potion
- Be cursed by holy person
- Drink water from werewolf's footprint
- Put on wolfskin belt
- Sleep outside, under a full moon

I always seem to get peckish at full moon!

Monster baby?

Strange creatures with snarling faces and wolf-like fangs appear in myths from many different lands. Most famous are 'were-jaguars' – half human, half jaguar – from the Olmec civilisation of Central America. They loved rain, not blood!

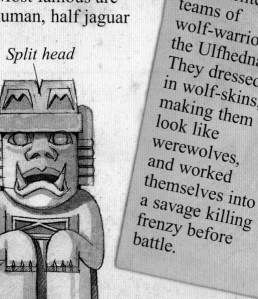

Split head

Snarling mouth

Hands like paws

Olmec stone carving of were-jaguar made around 1000 BC.

Wolf warriors

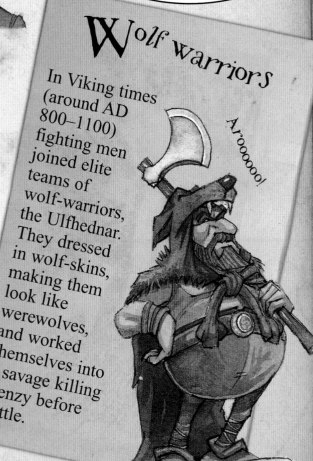

In Viking times (around AD 800–1100) fighting men joined elite teams of wolf-warriors, the Ulfhednar. They dressed in wolf-skins, making them look like werewolves, and worked themselves into a savage killing frenzy before battle.

Arooooo!

23

No 3

Medusa the Gorgon

Hiss!

Spit!

Look at me when I'm talking to you!

Medusa was born beautiful, with wonderful wavy hair. But she dared to say that she looked as good as the goddess Athene. Outraged, Athene turned Medusa's hair into snakes, her teeth into tusks and her hands into cold metal. Athene's final curse? Making Medusa's eyes turn men to stone. No-one would look at her now!

Vital statistics

Name: Gorgon
Appearance: Very ugly: staring eyes, lolling tongue, ghastly grin
Size: Tall woman
Armed with: Snakes, tusks, bronze hands, golden wings
Home: Ancient Greece
Powers: Deadly gaze

You wouldn't want to know this:

Just one drop of Medusa's blood could kill. It was also used as powerful – but dangerous – medicine.

Be prepared!
Always expect the very worst

Aha! Gotcha!

Mirror, mirror

How can you kill a Gorgon without being turned to stone? Greek hero Perseus used his shield as a mirror so his eyes wouldn't meet Medusa's gaze, and he cut off her head!

Awful warning

The Greek goddess Athene wore Medusa's head on the front of her armour. It sent out an awful warning: 'I'm mighty and dangerous! Keep away!' Gorgon heads were carved on Greek temples, too, to stop evil spirits entering.

What's in a name?

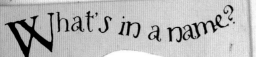

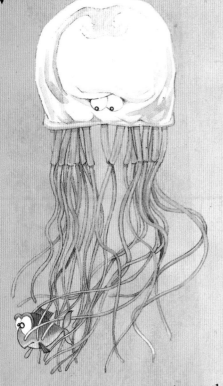

Some kinds of jellyfish have the name 'Medusa' because their long, trailing tentacles look like her snaky hair.

Don't look now!

Like Medusa, the Basilisk killed with a single glance. A very strange creature, it was hatched by a rooster from a serpent's egg, spat fire, and trailed poisonous slime.

Cluck!

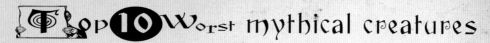

 No 2

Vampire

Dead but undead! Vampires cannot rest in peace, but haunt the world of the living, longing for fresh blood. Greed and violence are their only pleasures; they do not care how many they devour. Loathed and feared, they are outcasts forever – unless they are caught and killed (again!) in horrid and revolting ways.

Sinister cloak, like bat's wings

Mwahahaha!

Come closer! Very close! There's nothing to fear...

Vital statistics

Name: Vampire

Appearance: Deathly pale (or dark red); burning eyes, hairy palms

Size: From thin and hungry to bloated and swollen

Armed with: Fangs, claws, sinister smile

Home: Primarily Eastern Europe, but also worldwide

Powers: Bloodsucker!

You wouldn't want to know this:

Just one bite from a vampire will make you a vampire too.

Be prepared!
Always expect the very worst

Evil omen

Roman myths told how the Strix (screech owl) was once a woman, but she ate human flesh and blood, and became a vampire bird.

Screeeeech!

Seeing the Strix brought bad luck.

Vampire~proof?

Vampires hate garlic and can't cross running water. The best advice? Don't let them near enough to kiss – or bite – you!

Worldwide horror

Vampire myths come from many lands. In Mexico, the Aztec Cihuateotl (Night Demon) stole children, sent madness and drank blood.

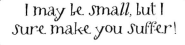

I may be small, but I sure make you suffer!

Mighty Bite!

Vampires are not the only creatures to suck blood. Tiny insects, such as moquitoes and bed-bugs (*pictured right*), also feast on it. Their bites itch, bleed and spread dangerous diseases. Ugh!

Itch!

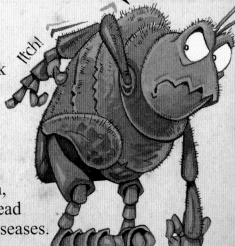

27

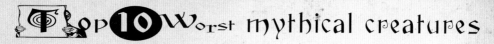

№1

Dragon

Marvel or monster? The dragon is both. Its size, strength and wisdom give it great powers to help or do harm. In Chinese myths, dragons mostly guard and guide – though they are awesomely awful when angry. Elsewhere in the world, dragons mean danger. They snatch and swallow victims, and their fiery breath destroys whole kingdoms. They also smell foul!

Chinese dragon

Roar!

Vital statistics

Name: Dragon (Chinese)
Appearance: Snake with legs
Size: Small as a silkworm, big as the world
Armed with: Sharp teeth and claws
Home: Up among rainclouds in the sky
Powers: Control the weather; guard emperors; become invisible; glow in the dark.

You wouldn't want to know this:

Angry dragons send disastrous tsunamis and floods.

Be prepared!
Always expect the very worst

Devil in disguise

Outside China, dragons are fierce, cruel devils. They delight in evil, and kill to win hoards of golden treasure.

It's mine! All mine!

Many-headed monster

Greek myths tell how hero Heracles fought the Hydra, a hundred-headed dragon. As he sliced heads off with his sword, more grew to replace them.

Hisss!

Spit!

Dragon of doom

Jormungandr, the World Serpent, appears in myths from Viking lands. He wraps himself round the world, holding his tail in his mouth. When he lets go, the world will end!

Grrrr!

England's hero?

George, the patron saint of England, is famous for killing a dragon. But his story is a myth, in praise of courage. George probably never lived – but nor did dragons!

Stab!

Glossary

Ancestor A blood relative who lived many, many years ago.

Ancient Referring to something that existed before the Middle Ages, the 5th century AD.

Athene (also Athena) The Ancient Greek goddess of wisdom and strength.

Bronze A metal made of copper and tin.

Corpse The dead body of a human or animal.

Cyberspace Another word for the World Wide Web, the immense collection of websites brought together by the Internet.

Emperor The ruler of an empire.

Fangs Long, pointed teeth often found in meat-eating animals and also in fantasy creatures like vampires and dragons.

Goral A goat-like animal found in different parts of Asia.

Guardian Someone or something that looks after, or guards, a precious item, person or animal.

Himalayas A vast mountain range which stretches across six countries in Asia.

Hoax A trick played on people to make them believe something that isn't true.

Hybrid A combination of two or more different things.

Hydra The many-headed water beast which was killed by the Ancient Greek hero Heracles.

Inquisitive Liking to ask a lot of questions.

Israelites In the Bible, the descendants of Jacob.

Jaguar A big cat found in North and South America.

Labyrinth In Ancient Greek mythology, the maze that was built to hold the Minotaur.

Manatee (or sea cow) A large friendly mammal that lives in the sea.

Monastery A building, or group of buildings, which is the home of a community of monks.

Myth A story told in ancient times, often associated with religion.

Pliosaur A type of reptile that lived under the sea in prehistoric times.

Poison A substance that is harmful if eaten, drunk or absorbed through the skin.

Prehistoric The period of time before recorded history.

Prey A creature that is killed for food.

Sacrifice A living creature that is killed in order to please or to calm the gods.

Silkworm A very small caterpillar which produces silk.

Slavering Slobbering or drooling saliva from the mouth.

Sling A folded piece of cloth used to throw something by swinging it.

Talons Sharp claws.

Tentacles Long, trailing body-parts of sea creatures that often have stings, suckers or hooks.

Tsunami A huge and destructive wave of water.

Wingspan The distance between the tip of one wing and the tip of the other.

Thunderbird

Top 10 Worst mythical creatures

Index